Yachats

The Town Called "Dark Water At the Foot of the Mountains."

George R. Mead

E-Cat Worlds Press

Comments and questions? –> gmead01@gmail.com

Yachats
Copyright 2012 by George R. Mead

All rights reserved. No part of this document may be reproduced, stored in a retrieval system, or transmitted, in any form or by an means, electronic, mechanical, photocopying, or otherwise, with out prior permission of E-Cat Worlds Press. This includes a prohibition on rebinding.

LCCN 2012946943

Mead, George R.
/Yachats. The Town Called "Dark Water At the Foot of the Mountains."
George R. Mead.
ISBN-13 978-0-9817446-9-8
1. History. 2. Oregon

E-Cat Worlds established its publishing program as a reaction to the large commercial publishing houses currently dominating the book industry and the smaller intellectual clones. It is interested in publishing works of fiction and non-fiction that are often deemed insufficiently profitable or commercial or that are not necessarily reflective of current literary trends and fads.

E-Cat Worlds, 57744 Foothill Road, La Grande OR 97850
www.ecatworldspress.com
SAN 255-6383

Cover Photo - Eastyn Mead, Boise , Idaho

In the middle of nowhere - Creativity.

First Edition:
Printed in the United States of America

Fiction

From Grandeville.

Portal
Lair
Search
Not Again
And Again.
Magiwitch
Rebirth
Offspring
Holiday
Treasure
E'Nilt
Briadna

A Tale of the Feyra

Jonathon and Dee
Dee of The Fontala
Dee and The People

Nonfiction

A History of Union County
The Ethnobotany of the California Indians
A History of the Chinese in The West: 1848-1880.
Yachats. The Town Called "Dark Water at the Foot of the Mountains."

There are many histories written. They are, most often, histories of "big" events or places. By "big" I mean that there are lots of histories of The Civil War and all the others wars the United States has been involved in. There are numerous histories, or biographies, of people that are of "commercial" interest, such as: Generals, movie stars, short-term personalities, large cities, etc.

But there are very few histories of the small places that are more than the usual compilation of folk beliefs or just so stories. The problem with these kinds of historical "knowledge" is that they are dependent upon memories of, frequently, long ago events, or remembrances of what members several generations ago said to their children and/or grandchildren. These remembrances become anecdotal stories that frequently have little or no reference to actual events nor do they reflect those actual events. They are often not very good as to accuracy or to occurrence.

Small histories, such as this one, are hard to write because they are hard to document. Folk tend to not keep those things that would verify their own history, especially for small places or events. This makes it difficult to find something that the reader can find and read for themselves, to verify what is herein discussed.

Today and Quite Some Time Ago

Walking along the trail that wanders between the various dwellings (houses and hotels) that line the edge between Yachats and the ocean one watches the waves breaking over the dark stone and wonders about wind, waves, and the ocean-land interface.

What one sees today is all a matter of continental drift, what is now called plate tectonics. The term continental drift was coined by Alfred Wegener. He was born 1 November 1880 in Berlin and died sometime after 19 October 1930, the exact date is unknown as he was on an expedition to Greenland to monitor arctic weather for a 12-month period. His body was only found six months after the start of that activity on 12 May 1931.

Wegener first thought of what he called "continental drift" when he noticed that various of the large land masses appeared to fit together much like pieces in a cross-word puzzle, especially visible between Africa and South America. He found physical evidence, mainly in fossil plants, that indicated to him that at one time these land masses were joined and suggested his theory in 1921. While he presented a large amount of evidence in support of his concept he couldn't find a mechanism to support it.

The accepted wisdom of the day, as most often happens, denied such a thing as possible and so it remained until fairly recently.

By the 1950s the data derived from studies of the deep sea floor finally provided what was needed to bring Wegener's idea to the fore, although now the view had shifted from continental drift to plate tectonics as a more accurate label for what the earth's crust was actually doing. A series of papers written in the time period 1965-1967 demonstrated how feasible the idea was and defined the theory which today is understood as the norm.

It is generally recognized that there are two kinds of crust, the continental crust, and the oceanic crust (as an over-generalized explanation). Continental crust is inherently lighter having a different composition than the oceanic crust. Both reside above the much deeper fluid mantel of the planet.

There are seven or eight large continental plates (depending upon how they are defined) of which the one of concern for our discussion is the North American Plate. In addition there are dozens of smaller plates, one of the larger among the seven largest of the smaller, is the Juan de Fuca Plate.

The Juan de Fuca Plate, named after the explorer, is subducting (essentially bending and sliding under) the northern portion of the western edge of the North American Plate. This process has formed the Cascade Range, the Cascade Volcanic Arc, and the Pacific Ranges which run from southern British Columbia to northern

California.

Volcanic activity as a result of these two plates sliding, one over the other, produced, about 66 million years ago, great flows of basalt which take their shape as a result of hot basalt rapidly being cooled upon meeting the ocean water into which it was flowing into formations, often called "pillow" lava. These formations produced offshore were then pushed into the continental plate and forced upward to create the western edge of Oregon.

Over time, as the ocean level rose and fell during the ice age, the shoreline moved back and forth, relative to the land, cutting sea terraces into the land by removing the softer materials and leaving the dark basalt formations exposed. Weak spots in the basalt formation produced the cracks seen today where the waves pour in and produce the dramatic explosions of water all enjoy watching.

So, while strolling along the seashore trail this brief account of the geological change that produced the current environment can answer, to some degree, the question(s) often asked as to why the current shoreline, cracks and all, came to be the way it is.

Those Who Came First

The following discussion is mainly based upon the work of Beckham (1977), Kittel and Curtis (1996), Whereat (2010), and Wilkinson (2010).

The Alsea (also spelled at times Alsee, Alseya) the label most often used today, a corruption of Wooshea, the native name given to the Alsee River Valley, were in the area perhaps between 8,000-6,000 years ago, maybe more recently when the Oregon shoreline began to take on its present configuration.

Their ancestors had wandered into the New World from the Old World during that period of time when there was dry land connecting eastern Siberia and western Alaska. Beringia, as it is called, was one of the land bridges that appeared when the level of the ocean fell during the most recent ice age. The four land bridges that appeared were: 1) Beringia; 2) a connection between Australia, New Guinea, and Tasmania; 3) the British Isles connecting to continental Europe; and, 4) the Asian mainland connecting with Sumatra, Java, and Borneo.

Folk could cross Beringia from around 14,000

years ago until about 10,500 years ago when the melting of the ice once again caused sea levels to rise and cover this area and the others. When the sea level had previously dropped an estimated 300 feet or so, the area of Berginia was roughly equivalent to twice the size of the State of Texas.

The Alsea, who lived in and around this area (Yachats), were known to have villages along the ocean and on the edges of the bays. The lands of the Alsea had, as did other areas up and down the Oregon Coast, deer, elk, bear, waterfowl, seals, sea lions, shellfish of many varieties, as well as edible plants such as camas, wild berries, etc.

They were here long before the West Coast of Oregon and the other western states were "discovered" by the non-Indians: British, Spanish, Russian, and American. Unfortunately for the indigenous population these folk from elsewhere brought with them a very strange idea that dated from about the fifth century in Europe. They believed in the idea of what they called the "right of discovery." In their minds land that was "found" and not already inhabited by any of the others who believed in the same thing that they did allowed them the right to claim and use the "found" land for themselves regardless of who might already be living there (previous to these newcomers "finding" it).

There was a band of the Alsea located on or near the Yachats River as well as just north of modern-day Yachats. They built semi-subterranean houses with walls and roofs constructed from cedar planks. The remains of most of these structures were destroyed or buried by recent construction, ca. 1951. Archaeological testing of various Indian sites suggests that there was a seasonal occupation in the general area of Yachats at least back to 1,500 years ago. Beads found in some of the sites are dated as recent as 1790-1820, not too much earlier than the mass migration of non-Indians into Oregon. Charcoal found in one site dated to 4,770 years ago puts the age of the site right on the edge of the dating for the change in sea level from 10,000 to 5,000 years ago when the Oregon Coast took on its present appearance.

It is estimated that the Coos, Siuslaw, Lower Umpqua, and Alsea totaled around 7,600 people before contact.

The Alsea covered an area that stretched from the Alsee River in the north to Tenmile Creek which is just south of Sedrace, a territory that includes today's Yachats and Cape Perpetua.

Contact between the coast tribes and the movement of the non-Indian populations into the region was totally detrimental to these indigenous peoples. Between the foreign diseases that were brought into the region by these new folk (tuberculosis, smallpox, measles, to list a few of the worse) and the political games played by the politicians, the Alsea and many others were mostly eliminated. The killing diseases may have entered Oregon as early as the 1520s. It is certainly true that diseases struck by the 1770s and at least every decade from the 1770s through the 1850s.

The Alsea population was reduced by 94%.

Congress passed the Oregon Donation Act (a misnomer if there ever was one) on 29 September 1850 which allowed them to disperse the tribe's property regardless of any other law currently on the books. This law promised 300 acres free to every settler 18 years or older who had lived in Oregon by December 1851. 7,437 claims were filed in western Oregon taking 2,500,000 acres out of the Indians land base. In 1855 when the Coast (Siltez) Reservation was established it originally stretched 105 miles north to south, from Cape Lookout to the divide between the Siuslaw and Umpqua Rivers, running 23 miles inland in the south and 12 miles in the north. The reservation was created by an Executive Order by President Franklin Pierce but Congress never ratified the treaty. This meant that over time problems were created for generations of western Oregon Indians due to arguments over forms of legalities relating to the status of the reservation.

The President of the United States signed an Executive Order, 21 December 1865, which cut the Siletz Reservation into two parts ripping a large hole through the middle of the reservation thirty-two kilometers wide by forty kilometers long giving all of the Yaquina Bay and The Alsea estuary to white settlers. This decision removed 200,000 acres, about one fifth of the then current reservation, more than 300 square miles for which the Indians received no compensation.

The Alsea Sub-agency, built by Indian laborers, was established 3 September 1859 to hold the remnants of the Alsea, Siuslaw, Coos, and Lower Umpqua people. The board houses, storage buildings, and agricultural fields were located at Agemcu Creek, near the location of the modern day Adobe Motel in Yachats. This decision was due to the actions of the Superintendent of Indian Affairs in Oregon to close the Umpqua Sub-agency. He had the new agent, J.B. Sykes, bring the Coos and the Lower Umpqua on a forced march 80 miles from Coos Bay to Yachats. In 1863 the Indian population at the Agency was recorded as 525 of which 150 were Alsea, by 1873 the total population was 343. The Alsea Indians of the Yahuch band who had lived in the Yachats area before the creation of the agency died from disease thirty years before the agency was established (as told in some accounts to early investigators of the local Indian cultures). The 1910 Census listed 29 or so individuals. By the 1930 Census this population was reduced to 9.

Sam Case was the agent from 1870 to February 1872, and then again from 23 March 1873 to June 1873. His daughter, Ida L. Case Ingells was born in 1871 at the Sub-agency becoming the first non-Indian born in the area. Case moved north and claimed the west end of the bay and named it Newport and became involved in educational and town development. He died in 1897. Sam Case Elementary school in Newport is named after him.

The United States government, including Senator John Mitchell from Oregon, decided to close the Alsea sub-agency in order to open the land for homesteading with an Act of Congress, 3 March 1875, stating "Indians shall not be removed from their present reservation without their [Indians] consent."

John Mitchell was first elected in 1872 to the Senate and was there until his death in 1905. His primary belief was that the interests of business and the interests of the national government were the same. He urged the closure of the Alsea Sub-agency as a money saving measure while at the save time favoring the interests of the lumber companies and others wishing to gain lands currently held by the Indians.

None consented. Yet Siltz Agent Simpson (then the Federal Surveyor General of Oregon) reported that they had given their consent even though they had not. The Alsea sub-agency was disbanded in 1875. At the same time an additional 700,000 acres were removed from the Siletz Reservation bringing the reservation down to 225,000 acres. Then in 1894 the Congress of the United States approved an act that took 179,000 acres of the "surplus lands" of the reservation to be thrown open for the acquisition of non-Indians.

Overall, this process was merely a continuation of "the right of discovery" idea brought to the New World by emigrants from the Old World.

Yachats

Lincoln County was created on 20 February, 1893, from a piece of the southern end of Tillamook County and the western end of Benton County (Stephan 1968).

The creation of the county was a result of one very irritated lawyer, Ben Jones (Benjamin Franklin Jones, b 24 February 1858, d 9 March 1925) and the behavior of the rather ethnocentric politicians in the then county seat of Benton County, Corvallis. Jones headed a delegation that traveled to the county seat to ask for lumber for road improvement in his coastal area. Someone apparently suggested that: "Cherry poles would be good enough for you clam diggers down there." It appears the eastern portion of Benton County felt that the western edge, thinly populated, could be ignored as they had little political influence. Jones returned and began a campaign to create a new county. In 1893, State Senator C. B. Crosno, Lee Wade, and Ben Jones worked to do this. Crosno introduced Bill 119 which would create Bay County. Eventually the swing vote came from Senator Cogswell of Lake County who agreed to vote for the bill to create a new county if they would name the county after Abraham Lincoln (News-Times 1993; LCHS n.d.). The 1900 Census of Lincoln

County listed a population of 3,575.

Jones earned a law degree at Oregon Agricultural College and was admitted to the Oregon Bar in 1897. He eventually became a member of the state legislature as a representative of Lincoln and Polk counties. He died 9 March 1925 of a heart attack (Blakely 2006).

Ben Jones interest in the roads didn't end with the creation of Lincoln County. In 1919 he wrote the first bill, as a State Representative, that authorized the construction of the "Oregon Coast Highway" (HB 147). State Senator Al W. Norblad of Clatsop worked with Jones on this measure (Hays 1976). The measure was placed on the ballot and voted in by a 2-1 margin. Work was begun on this road in 1921, now called "The Roosevelt Coast Military Highway." The State of Oregon decided it would pass a bond measure for $2,500,00 if the Federal Government would appropriate a like amount (New York Times 1919). It was later renamed "The Oregon Coast Highway" (OCZMA 2008). The Oregon Coast Highway was finished in 1936.
[see Blakely 2006 for a detailed discussion of the construction of the Oregon Coast Highway.]

In 1913 Oregon had a total of 25 miles of paved road. Roads on this edge of the west coast of Oregon were minimal at best, often rough graded, wood plank, or crushed rock (ODOTHC 1999; OCZMA 2008). In 1926 the Oregon Highway Commission had noted that all roads leading to the coast were impassible after the first rains (OSHC ca. 1940's). An 1920 Oregon Road Map

(Blakely 2006) shows neither Yachats nor a road leading to the Yachats area. In 1929 there was only a single lane dirt road between Waldport and Yachts (Blakely 2006).

Before Lincoln County was created folk had been moving in and around the area that was to become the town of Yachats. The Ludemans and the Bobells who had immigrated from Germany to Minnesota relocated to Oregon and homesteaded farms on the upper Yachats River. In 1888 the Ludeman's built a fishing structure on pilings near Green Point, about a quarter mile from Waldport (Hennessey 2005). Other settlers moved into the area at the mouth of the Yachats and named their place Ocean View, or perhaps, Oceanview. This began to happen shortly after the closing of the Alsea Sub-agency in 1875. Some of the settlers noted in an account written around 1930 by the Rev. Virgil Howell (1880-1943) were Ingram on the present Carson place (ca. 1930), Robert Mann (1877-1945), Austin Howel, Bill Reaves, Harmon Buoy (1838-1903). Noting the few birth dates given by Howell it appears that they either arrived as children or some time later than the very earliest folk. The Buoy's moved to Lincoln County in 1872 and then to Yachats in 1884. Ms. Buoy was the first school teacher in Yachats. Virgil Howell was named the District Elder at the Free Methodist Conference, 26 Feb 1937. The group was also called the Oregon Free Methodists, at least in newspaper accounts of the time (The Morning Oregonian 1936; The Oregonian 1937).

During the 1880s and 1890s there were a number

of canneries operated on the Alsea River. Harrison, Freeman, and Dodge built the first one in 1886. Nice and Polemus built the Lutgens Cannery in 1887 further up the bay on pilings across the bay from town. The Barnes Cannery was out from old town (Hennessey 2005).

On 5 November 1875 the first Post Office was established, George M. Starr, postmaster. It was located about one mile north of today's town near where the Alsea Sub-agency had been located.

It was discontinued 27 September 1893 and then reopened on 27 April 1904, Jenneta Kindred postmistress. In 1912 the Post Office was relocated to the Hosford residence near the mouth of the Yachats River.

A new Post Office was established 13 October 1916, Donna Beer, postmistress.

After the question was raised by town folk it was decided to rename the town Yachats as it was felt that there were too many other towns with similar names having "ocean" in their name. J. Kenneth Berry (1905-1931) is given credit for suggesting this name change in some of the accounts. Census records give his name as Kenneth J. Berry, birth date as 1906.

Yachats has at times been spelled as Yachaats, Yuhuts (Daily Capital Journal 1910). Hays (1976) lists additional forms of the name: Youitts, Youitz, Yawhick, Yahuck, Yahauts, Yahatc, Yahts, Yaqa'yik, and Yahach.

The name Yachats has been interpreted by various of the linguists that had been studying western Oregon Indian languages to mean "dark water at the foot of the mountains," or "little river with big mouth," or "as far as you can go along the beach."

Until 1890 when the first road was built there was only a horse trail linking the town with other areas.

> Two thirds of the distance from Florence to Waldport, on Alsea Bay, consists of horse trails (The Morning Oregonian 1902).

In 1914 the U.S. Forest Service blasted a road around Cape Perpetua and built a wooden bridge over the Yachats River linking Yachats and the Florence area. The wooden bridge was replaced by a steel bridge, Montag and Sons contractors, for $23,034, in 1926. Until the road was rocked in 1931 rains made it impossible for the mail to be carried by automobile.

In 1909 the Yachats Telephone Company was created. The incorporators were O.V. Hurt, W.M. Brooks, and Silas Howel (Daily Capital Journal 1909).

The North Fork Yachats River Bridge, a covered bridge 38 feet long, was built in 1938. It was the last one constructed by veteran bridge builder Otis Hamer.

In 1917, 6 November, Brice P. Disque, newly promoted Colonel in the U.S. Army, Signal Corps, was given command of a new military unit called the Spruce Production Division, headquartered at the Yeon Building in downtown Portland. Sitka spruce, native to the coasts of Northern California, Oregon, Washington, British Columbia, and Alaska came into high demand in the production of airplanes for the war effort (World

War I). This wood has the combination of lightness, strength, resiliency, and long and tough fibre that made it the best of all other woods for this purpose. In addition it would not splinter when struck by a rifle bullet (Williams 1999).

Two miles north of Yachats this Division, having a territory roughly shaped as a parallelogram 400 miles long by 50 miles wide, built one of their sixty military logging camps which were usually located near existing privately owned sawmills. This camp was connected via rail to the town of Toledo. The mill at Toledo was 70% complete by November 11, 1918, when the war ended (U.S. Spruce Production Corporation n.d).

The Division initiated selected logging of the scattered spruce trees. Overall the Division built 13 railroads with over 173 miles of main line track and 181 miles of tributary or spur line. Seven of these lines were planned for Washington and six for coastal Oregon. At the peak of the construction there were 10,000 soldiers at work in this endeavor. The Spruce Division's use of truck and cars was the first large scale use of motor vehicles in the Pacific Northwest. The network of roads and railroads built by them opened the forests for future development of the logging industry and facilitated that growth for the remainder of the 20th century.

By early 1918 the Vancouver Barracks area, the old polo grounds across the Columbia River, became the location of the Cut-Up Plant, constructed and operated by spruce soldier labor. This sawmill became the largest spruce sawmill in the world producing more than one million feet of spruce lumber every day. The complex covered 50 acres and was operated by 2,400 soldiers of the Division. According to estimates the production of aircraft spruce increased 5,000 percent in little more than one year (United States Spruce Production Corporation n.d.). Overall the availability of spruce from the Northwest forests coupled with wartime developments in the aircraft industry simulated the Boeing Company and others to enter the commercial aircraft fleet.

One day after the Armistice was signed the Spruce Production Division stopped all activities. Equipment valued at over 12 million dollars was sold and stimulated the development of a number of private lumber companies (Williams 1999).

Camp One was then operated by the Manary Logging Company. It was about 2.8 miles north of Yachats close to the coast. The outfit shipped logs from there to Yaquina Bay by rail. This rail line was built by the military and known as Route XII or Alsea Southern from South Beach 24 miles south to the Camp One (United States Spruce Production Company n.d.). The camp, now in private hands, had several spurs lines into the Blodgett Timber Tract (13,440 acres) which stretched north from the Yachats River to about 1.5 miles above Camp One and east to the tall peaks of Yachats Mountain. The camp began operating in September 1922. It was owned by James Manary and his two sons, Gordon and Roland, as a subsidiary of the Pacific

Spruce Corporation. The Corporation had bought a large amount of the Spruce Production Division (timber, railroads, mill at Toledo) for two million dollars in December 1920 (Johnson 1924).

At Camp One, Manary had an office-house, store, warehouse, cook-house whose dining room was 18 x 100 feet with attached five bedrooms for the waitresses and special help, ten four-room bungalows, 24x30 feet, ten three-room bungalows, 4 bunkhouses, 20x60 feet, ten smaller bunk-houses, 12x20, a school house 24x36 feet. All water for the camp came from Divinity Creek through a gravity line to a 50,000 gallon holding tank on top of a 36 feet high wooden tower. Employees paid 40 cents per meal and 15 cents for bunkhouse accommodations.

Rev. Howell listed for the town of Yachats in 1930: two churches (the Evangelical and the Free Methodist), three grocery stores, two hotels, one bakery, a good school, a pool hall, and a large community hall.

Chittem Bark

In 1905/1906 the chittem bark warehouse (built in 1900) in Yachats was converted into the Yachats Hotel (Hays 1976).

So what is this stuff, chittem? The common term derives from Chinook Jargon: chitticum, chittam. The tree from which the bark comes is *Rhamnus Purshiana*, common name Cascara (Peck 1961). At times the botanical names were *Cuscuru sugrulu*, *Frangulu Purshiana*. It has also been called: Cascara buckthorn, scared bark tree, Oregon brearwood, bitterbark, coffeetree, coffeeberry, shittimwood, chittam, chittim, and buckthorn.

From about 1877 it was utilized as a laxative and became the principal ingredient in commercial, over-the-counter products. It had been utilized this way by the indigenous populations long before the settlers and others arrived. The main effect of the bark is that it induces the large intestine to increase its muscular contractions.

In the early 1900's gathering chittem bark was essentially a botanical gold rush in those areas where the tree grew.

> Corvallisites who went to Alsea and Yachats region to search for cascara homesteads are returning home. Cascara tree locators whom were to pay $50 for each quarter located failed to place them on lands that promised to justify the required outlay. None of those who returned has as yet filed homestead papers (Morning Oregonian 1903)
>
> Senator B.F. Jones, of Toledo, is among the speculators in cascara on a large tract of land on the Yachats, and will soon have a force of men at work
>
> * * * * *
>
> At but 10 cents per pound for the bark, the average workman can earn much more money stripping chittem bark than in the harvest field. This has caused many people to take up the work (Morning Oregonian 1904).

That the gathering of Cascara bark is becoming one of the important industries in Oregon is shown by the increased annual shipments of this drug from the state.

* * * * *

In May last, which marked the early part of ths season, the purchasing price averaged about 4 cents a pound. Subsequently the market gradually strengthened to 5 cents, and by the latter part of August it reached the 12 cent mark. Early in September the price advanced to 14 cents . . . (Daily Capital Journal 1904).

The cascara bark industry began, it is asserted, in California about 1865, and for many years California led in the production of bark, exporting as much as 50,000 pounds in a single year.

* * * * *

The forest experts say that the destructive methods practiced in obtaining the bark on privately owned land, has resulted in gradually reducing the abundance of cascara trees, leaving the National Forests as an important supplementary source of supply (The Bandon Recorder 1916).

On 9 May 2002, the U.S. Food and Drug Administration issued a final rule banning its use in the over-the-counter drug sales as frequent usage of chittem tended to be habit forming.

The Little Log Church

A small amount of religious history is required at

this point in our discussion.

In 1767 there was sweeping through the colonies of the time an inter-denominational renewal movement. During that time, Philip William Otterbein, a German Reformed minister met Martin Boehm, a Mennonite. The two of them created a movement which became named, in 1800, the United Brethren in Christ, and was apparently the first denomination to actually have begun in the United States. At about this same time a number of missionary movements were started in various of the churches: Congregationalists, Baptist, Presbyterians, and Methodists. As the United States spread westward, missionaries followed the flow of settlers and settlements (Behney and Eller 1979).

In 1861 the Pacific District was created by the United Brethren Church comprising California, Oregon, and the Walla Walla Conferences. The five bishop districts were rearranged to become four bishop districts east of the Rocky Mountains with the Pacific District to the west.

The church launched its first missionary venture, the "Home, Frontier, and Foreign Missionary Society," which sent a group from Indiana, under the leadership of T. J. Conner, a minster and a doctor, to Oregon to start United Brethren churches there. He was given $1,000 for expenses by the General Conference of 1853. This group of 98 people in 16 families, 38 oxen-pulled wagons, and 300 cattle spent five months on the trail. Another account states 30 wagons and nearly 100 people. Yet another account states 13 families numbering 80 people with others stating 15 families and 96 people (Buzzard 1988). They settled in the Willamette Valley in 1853 and became the nucleus of the Oregon Conference organized in 1853.

By 1889 the total church in the U.S. had grown to around 200,000 members and splint over arguments as to what their constitution allowed them to do. A small group of about 10,000 split away maintaining the more traditional view while the larger did not. The two groups became the Church of the United Brethren in Christ (the majority group) and The United Brethren Church (Old Constitution)(Behney and Eller 1979).

The Home, Frontier, and Foreign Missionary Society was broken into two separate operations in 1905: the Foreign Missionary Society, and the Home Missionary Society. The Home Missionary Society was dedicated to missionary activities in the United States and to church construction (Behney and Eller 1979).

The Evangelical Association, focused on missionary activity, sent missions to Oregon in 1864. The Oregon Mission was organized in 1855. The Pacific Conference was created in 1876. In 1883 the Pacific Conference was broken into the Oregon Conference and the California Conference. In 1888 the Oregon Conference broke their territory into the Washington district and the Oregon district (Poling1940).

In 1891 The Evangelical Association broke into two parts: The Evangelical Association (the majority) and the Evangelical Church (the minority) (Behney and

Eller 1979). The minority is also called the United Evangelical Church (Poling 1940).

In 1916 the Reverend Cook held revival meetings in Yachats (then know as Oceanview) (Hays 1976).

Prior to 1920, Yachats was served by visiting preachers due to the difficulty of travel up and down the coast. In 1922 the roving Reverend Rolla J. Phelps and his wife, Stella, both in their 50s, made a monthly trip from their home in Summit to Yachats along the road from Waldport to Yachats. The road often utilized the open beaches for access north and south (Wilson 2003). In 1927 they moved to the Bay View Mission of the Oregon Conference of the Evangelical Church. The Evangelical Association and the United Evangelical Church had been united in 1922 to become the Evangelical Church (Behney and Eller 1979). In Oregon they were called the Oregon Conference of the Evangelical Church (Poling 1940).

Rev. Phelps was the Missionary for the Bay View Mission of the Oregon Conference of the Evangelical Church that comprised Yachats, Alsea, and Bay View (Poling 1940). Phelps was a Probationer (license to preach, preacher on trail) in 1920, Deacon in 1923, retired in 1935, and died in 1962 (Buzzard 1988). Bay View is noted in the minutes of the 44th Annual Conference of the Evangelical Church (1927) and the 45th Annual Conference (1928) and then as Alsea-Yachats in the 46th Annual Conference (1929), the 47th (1930), the 48th (1931), the 49th (1932), all showing R. J.

Phelps. In the 50th (1933), 51st (1934), 52nd (1935), Yachats is listed as "Supply." In the 53rd (1936), J. Kenneth Wishart is listed. Donald Lentz is listed in the 54th (1937), then Yachats is "Supply" in the 55th (1938). The 55th Annual Conference minutes are the last listed by Poling (1940).

Rev. Phelps wanted to built a church in Yachats and is said to have received from The Mission Board of the Evangelical Church $200 for the project. Phelps stated (Phelps n.d.) that he paid the $200 for the lot upon which the church was constructed. Logs were donated and hauled down the Yachats River. Local volunteers cut cedar shakes as well as providing labor for the construction of the cross-shaped church building. It is said that the pews, windowpanes were donated to Yachats from a church in Philomath. Poling (1940) states that: "Material was used in its structure from Buelah church in Benton County." The Beulah church was located seven miles south of Corvallis. Death of and removal to other neighborhoods of its congregation ended in the church being torn down with materials being utilized in other areas (Poling 1940). Stella Phelps donated her small pump organ, dated 1907, to the church. The bell came from a Lentz church near Klamath Falls (Hays 1976). The church was dedicated in 1930.

When the congregation grew too large (then holding meetings in the Yachats Ladies Club Hall) the structure was given to the Lincoln County Historical Society (Hays 1976), or sold to the Lincoln County

Historical Society (Evans 1994), who later donated it to The City of Yachats in 1986 where it is now maintained as the Little Log Church and Museum.

The Friends of The Little Log Church was formed in 1991 (often called "The Willing Helpers").

In 1992 the church was closed due to safety regulations. There was no foundation. The logs were rotting on the ground. There were powder post beetles, carpenter ants, and termites in the wood. The church underwent complete restoration in 1993 with the City of Yachats donating $14,000 for the new foundation. In 1997, a 400-square-foot annex was constructed to hold local historical artifacts (Evans 1994; Hays 1975).

The Evangelical United Brethren Church came into being on 16 November 1946 when two churches were united: The Church of the United Brethren and the Evangelical Church (Behney and Eller 1979; Buzzard 1988). Thus the often quoted statement found in many discussions of this church that the early minsters were part of the Evangelical United Brethren Church are just plainly in error.

An often repeated statement that one sees about the building of the church is one that states: "Sir Robert Perks of England, who at that time owned most of Yachats, gave a parcel of his land for this worthy cause" (Hays 1976). This statement is often worded in various ways but the sense is always the same. It is interesting that this statement is both true and false at the same time.

Sir Robert William Perks, of London, England,

was involved with a number of public works, at home and abroad: the Barry Docks and Railways in South Wales; the Preston Docks and the Manchester Ship Canal; the great Harbor works at Buenos Aires, Argentina; a quay wall around Rio Bay, Brazil. He was an enthusiastic Methodist who felt that there was what seemed to him to be a innate ability for business among the Methodists. He wrote about an international bond of Christian unity and service for the Methodist Church. In the early 1900's he was often quoted in the Portland and other newspapers of the west. He traveled to the United States ca. 1907. He was elected to Parliament in 1892 (Crane 1909) and retired in 1910 stating: "there was no period of his life so fruitlessly spent, no time so absolutely wasted" (Covick 2008).

Unfortunately his biography stops in 1909 Cranfield 1909).

A search through the land transaction volumes at the Lincoln County Courthouse in Newport found the following transactions (full text in the appendix for each entry):

> 9 May 1927 - Lumbermans Trust selling to Sir Robert William Perks and Lady Edith Perks. (signed 9 May 1927; filed and recorded, 4 November 1927, 2:34 p.m.)
>
> 9 May 1927 - Sir Robert William Perks and Lady Edith Perks selling to the Equitable Trust Company (the renamed Lumbermans Trust). (signed 9 May 1927; filed and recorded, 4 November 1927, 2:36 p.m.)

10 Sept 1929 - The Equitable Trust selling to the Oregon Conference Evangelical Church of Oregon.

8 Aug 1952 - The Oregon Conference of Evangelical Church of Oregon selling to Willamette Presbytery Church.

Inside all these transactions one finds that the lot upon which the Little Log Church was built is included in the sales. There was no donation. The 9 May 1927 sale was a very large bundle of real estate in Yachats. So Perks did own a large piece of Yachats but only until he sold it back to the recreated Lumbermans Trust shortly after his purchase, apparently on the same day. What Phelps did with the $200 is unknown.

The 10 Sept 1929 sale has this as one of the conditions: "FIRST. *That said property shall be used and maintained for religious purposes only."* The sale price was $10.

The Lumbermans Trust was created in 1913.

> The Lumbermans Trust and Savings Bank has been organized in Portland, Ore., with practically the same stockholders as the Lumberman's National Bank.
>
> *   *   *   *   **
>
> The bond department of the Lumberman's National Bank has been transferred to the Trust and Savings Bank, which will give special attention to the investment bond business and will deal in bonds and mortgages (The New York Times 1913).

In 1914 it listed assets of $651,924.84 of which $459,852.48 were in loans (USM&TC 1914).

During the time period of 29 Sept 1923 to 12 Mar 1927, The Lumbermans Trust was heavily engaged in buying real estate.

Alvin Krech was the president for 20 years and since 1923 board chairman of the Equitable Trust (Time Magazine 1928). He was also the secretary of the Reorganization Committee for the Union Pacific Railroad, 1895-1906, during its period of insolvency. Given that The Equitable Trust Company was placed in the hands of a receiver around 1935 it may will be that was his job with The Equitable Trust as well.

During all the research I could find no obvious link between what was a rather small (in terms of economic worth) The Lumbersmans Trust/Equitable Trust and the very wealthy Sir Robert Perks. Both the deeds he was involved in were notarized in London which suggests that he was not in western Oregon during these transactions.

A nephew of Perks, George W. Volckman, was a representative of the McArthur-Perks Company, a major contractor for railroad construction in the United States, on the project connecting Coos Bay to the Central Valley, as well as other projects in western Oregon, in the early 1900s. Newspapers during this time sometimes referred to G. W. Volckman as Perks' nephew. Perks was also mentioned in various accounts as being quite wealthy (The Bandon Recorder 1916; The Coos Bay

Times 1911, 1913; The Malheur Enterprise 1912).

One might speculate that members of the Lumbersman Trust/Equity Trust contacted Volckman about some land transactions they needed to make and he in turn enlisted the aid of his uncle. Of course, this is mere speculation as I could not find anything that would support this idea other than coincidence.

Amanda's Trail

The trail, 3 1/4 miles in length, was dedicated on 19 July 2009. It climbs 800 feet from downtown Yachats to the summit of Cape Perpetua where it links to the trail system of the Siuslaw National Forest.

In ca. 1864 the U.S. Army forcibly removed and then herded the Coos and Lower Umpqua Indians from their lands in order to open the area for white settlers. They force marched their prisoners 80 miles north to the Alsea sub-Agency at Yachats.

According to the stories told of that time, a young, blind, Coos woman named Amanda De-Cuys, the common-law wife of a white settler who refused to marry her, was grabbed by the troops and hauled away, from her child and common-law husband. The soldiers were allowed to take any common-law spouse without regard to the situation or the damage done to families (Kittel and Curtis 1996).

Amanda, being blind, was bound to others for guidance as the troop forced all their captives to walk, barefoot or otherwise, over the jagged rock of the trail and though blackberry thickets with no regard as to the health and well being of the Indians.

The trail was named by Lloyd Collette, who worked for the Siuslaw National Forest in the 1970s and designed the initial trail route. The route was altered by a donation of some of the 27 acres owned by Joanne and Norman Kittel.

The trail was completed with the involvement and cooperation of the Siuslaw National Forest, Oregon States Parks, the Lincoln Land Legacy, Angel Job Corps, the Oregon Youth and Conservation Corps, View the Future, Kathleen and Jerry Sand, and the past mayor of Yachats, Susanne Smith, and the efforts of Joanne Kittel.

The 804 Trail.

This 804 road was established in 1890 as a road along the route utilized since 1875 by the stage, freight hauling, and the U.S. Mail. It came into existence when a group of Yachats farmers appealed to the county commissioners for a route to link Waldport and Yachats (Register-Guard 2004).

Developers asked the county to vacate a three-quarter mile piece of the road and barricaded sections of what they called the "ghost trail" from public access.

> The Citizens of this area are almost unanimously opposed to the vacation of this road (Benson 1974).
>
> Lincoln County commissioners voted unanimously to deny petitions to vacate a portion of 804 road in Yachts (Newport News-Times

1974).

The Committee To Save Yachats 804 Road Trail, Inc., was formed by 300 citizens, 7 July 1977. They were reacting against the development of various proposed recreation vehicle parks and condominiums on the oceanfront property north of Smelt Sands State Wayside.

On 14 November 1985, the Court of Appeals stated that: "The public has a right to walk the bluff in Yachats overlooking the ocean."

The Oregon Supreme Court upheld the public access, 12 November 1986.

The Lincoln County commissioners transferred the ownership of the road to the State of Oregon.

The Oregon Parks & Recreation Department took over the development and maintenance of the road-turned-trail on 18 July 1990 (MS and newspaper clippings in the Little Log Cabin archives).

It took active work on the part of the Citizen's Committee to prevent various real estate interests from closing access to both the old road route and the shoreline. They worked from 1977 until 1990 before the matter was finally settled.

The trail is now part of the Oregon Coast Trail system.

Gerdemann Botanic Preserve.

James (Jim) Wessel Gerdemann, Ph.D.-Plant Pathology, and his wife Janice moved to the Yachats' area in 1981 after he retired from the University of Illinois. They purchased an acre of hemlock and spruce that bordered the Siuslaw National Forest. They collected unusual plants, adapting them to the microclimate on their property. Over time their holdings grew to 3.5 acres.

In October 2002, Jerry and Kathleen Sand purchased the property with an irrevocable conservation easement which insures that the entire garden remains intact as a living legacy of its creators.

The plant collection includes, the native Sitka Spruce and Western Hemlock along with introduced plants such as: New Zealand tree ferns, Australian Grevilla, Chilean Flame and Lantern tree.

The Preserve has a public footpath which is open during daylight hours, no dogs are allowed. There is no parking available at either end of the footpath (see gerdemanngarden.org for news and other details).

Yachats Community Park.

In the city center is a restored marshland with boardwalks and paths through the area. Here one can see preserved spruce forest, a variety of native plants, and the wild life that visits, including migrating waterfowl, and ospreys that nest on the nest platforms. There is a picnic shelter, peace garden, and benches to sit on.

The Yachats Community Park Task Force spent four years in planning, research, and searching for funding to order to be able to restore the area (see www.ci.yachats.or.us/special/Yachats_Park_Brochure-sm.pdf).

The Grocery Store/Market.

"Murphys established the first store in 1900 " (Hays 1976).

In 1938, Fredericks Store - Grocers & Fresh Meats advertised in the short-lived Yachats Times, begun in June 1938, published on Saturdays (Hays 1976).

The Yachats Village Market, run by Jerry Clark and three generations of his family, was closed when the new owner (Bend-based Audia Moore Properties LLC, owner Jay Audias), who bought the market in January 2007, went out of business (in 2007) owing at least $1.5 million for properties in Waldport and Yachats (The Register-Guard 2010). Local residents banded together to get groceries to those who couldn't drive to Waldport setting up a hot line for those that required help.

The market reopened as part of the C&K Market chain when that company leased the property and revamped it. The store was planned to open in June 2010 (The Oregonian 2010).

The Yachats Commons.

The building was built in the 1930s and used as a school until 1983. The building was bought by the city and houses the city government office and a number of activities overseen by the Friends of the Yachats Commons Foundation. Among the activities held in The

Commons are Yachats Movie Night, the Farmers Market (May - October), art and crafts shows.

The Yachats Academy of Arts & Sciences sponsor speakers, films, workshops, exhibitions, and seminars in the Commons as well.

The Yachats Public Library.

The library was established in November 1973 by Ordinance 36: "The City of Yachats does hereby establish a public library to be known as the 'Yachats Public Library' to be operated and funded by the said city and to be used for the educational and cultural benefit by the citizens of the said city in accordance with the rules and regulations of the said library."

The library is operated and managed entirely by volunteers and Library commission members.

The library has a perpetual exhibit of paintings, drawings, and photographs by the Yachats Arts Guild with the exhibits changing every few weeks or so. The Yachats Seed Bank is housed in the library and provides vegetable seeds for free to gardeners. The library has a wide selection of cookbooks, gardening manuals, etc., as well.

References

Beckham, Stephen Dow
    1977   The Indians of Western Oregon. This Land Was Theirs. Coos Bay, OR: Arago Books.

Behney, J. Bruce and Paul H. Eller
    1979   The History of the Evangelical United Brethren Church (ed. Kenneth W. Krueger). Nashville TN: Abington.

Benson, Virgil I.
    1974   Copy of a letter written 6 April 1974. MS on file, The Little Log Church Museum.

Blakely, Joe. R.
    2006   Lifting Oregon Out of the Mud. Building the Oregon Coast Highway. Eugene OR: CraneDance Publications.

Buzzard, Theodore R.
    1988   Lest We Forget. A History of the Evangelical United Brethren Church in the Pacific Northwest. Portland OR: Theodore R. Buzzard.

Covick, Owen E.
> 2008 R W Perks and the Barry Railroad Company, Part 2: enter R W Perks. *Journal of the Railway & Canal Historical Society*, 203, 141-152.

Cranfield, Walter Thomas
> 1909 The Life-Story of Sir Robert W. Perks, Baronet. London: Charles H. Kelly.
> [Cranfield, a journalist, wrote this work under the pen name of Denis Crane in 1909 - the work, the copy that I have, is a reprint readily available which is listed under the Cranfield name.]

Daily Capital Journal (Salem, OR)
> 26 June 1909
> 5 January 1910

Evans, Shelia
> 1994 Yachat's Little Log Church. *Oregon Coast* March/April 1994.

Hays, Marjorie H.
> 1975 History of The Church: The 25th Anniversary of the Presbyterian Church, Yachats, Oregon. MS on file in The Little Log Church Museum.

1976 The Land That Kept Its Promise. A History of South Lincoln County. Newport: Lincoln County Historic Society (Publication No. 14).

Hennessey, Jennifer Taylor
    2005 A Historical Reconstruction and Land Use History of Six Tidal Wetlands in Oregon. Masters of Science Project, Marine Resource Management, College of Oceanic and Atmospheric Science, Oregon State University. Corvallis OR.

Johnson, Bolling Arthur (ed)
    1924 Pacific Spruce Corporation and Subsidiaries. C.D. Johnson Lumber Company. Manary Logging Company. Pacific Spruce Northern Railway Co. Chicago, IL: *Lumber World Review*, February 10, 1924.

Kittel, Joanna, and Suzanne Curtis
    1996 The Yachats Indians, Origins of the Yachats Name, and the Prison Camp Years. (Revised 2010). Confederated Tribes of Coos, Lower Umpqua, and Siuslaw Indians, and the Confederated Tribes of Siletz Indians of Oregon.

LCHS (Lincoln County Historical Society)
n.d. A Short History of Lincoln County, Oregon. Ms of file. Lincoln County Historical Society.

New York Times
1913 Starts Auxiliary Bank. Lumberman's of Portland, Ore., Follows Examples of the East. July 18, 1913.

Newport News-Times (Newport, OR).
12 September 1974 (Thurs)

News-Times
1993 The First 100 Years. Lincoln County. Newport OR: The News-Times.

Peck, Morton Eaton
1961 A Manual of the Higher Plants of Oregon, 2nd Edition. Oregon State University Press.

Phelps, Rolla J.
n.d MS on file. The Little Log Church Museum. Yachats.

Poling, C. C.
1940 History of the Evangelical Church in Oregon and Washington 1864-1938. Portland, OR: Loomis Printing Company.

Stephan, G. Edward
> 1968   Intra-State Boundaries: A Set of Historical Maps Showing the Development of County Government in Oregon. Eugene OR: University of Oregon.

The Bandon Recorder (Bandon, OR)
> 06 June 1916

The Coos Bay Times (Marshfield, OR)
> 01 October 1913
> 14 October 1911

The Malheur Enterprise (Vale, OR)
> 22 June 1922

The Morning Oregonian Portland, OR)
> 1 September 1902
> 9 October 1903
> 22 April 1904
> 21 July 1936

The Oregonian (Portland, OR)
> 26 July 1937
> 17 April 2010

The Register-Guard (Eugene, OR)
> 81 Oct 2004
> 12 January 2010

Time Magazine
> 1928 Business: Death of Krech. Monday, May 14, 1928.

United States Spruce Production Corporation
> (N. D. -> perhaps 1920?)
>> History of Spruce Production Division, United State Army and United States Spruce Production Corporation. Portland, OR: Press of Kilham Stationary & Printing Co.

USM&TC
> 1914 Trust Companys of the United States 1914. New York: United States Mortgage & Trust Company.

Whereat, Don (editor)
> 2010 The Confederated Tribes of the Coos, Lower Umpqua and Siuslaw Indians. Our Culture and History.

Wilkinson, Charles
> 2010 The People Are Dancing Again. The History of the Siletz Tribe of Western Oregon. Seattle: The University of Washington Press.

Williams, Gerald W.
    1999   The Spruce Production Division. *Forest History Today Magazine* (Spring 1999). The Forest History Society.

Wilson, Robert
    2003   Gem of the Oregon Coast. Yachats. The Story of Yachats Told in Poetic Essays. Yachats, OR: Overleaf Publishing and Marketing.

Appendix

Note: all the spelling and punctuation are as they occurred in the deeds as recorded.

9 May 1927 - Lumbermans Trust selling to Sir Robert William Perks and Lady Edith Perks.

Deed   A 12450

KNOW ALL MEN BY THESE PRESENT, That LUMBERMANS TRUST COMPANY, a corporation organized and existing under and by virtue of the laws of the State of Oregon, in consideration of Ten Dollars ($ 10.00) and other consideration to it paid by SIR ROBERT WILLIAM PERKS, of London, England, has bargained and sold unto said SIR WILLIAM PERKS, his heirs and assigns, all the following bounded and described parcels of real property, situated in the County of Lincoln and State of Oregon, to-wit:

<u>Parcel No: 1.</u> Lot numbered Three (3) in section Twenty two (22);

<u>Parcel No. 2</u> Southwest quarter of Southwest quarter of Section Three (23):

<u>Parcel No. 3</u> West half of Northwest quarter of Section Twenty-six (26):

<u>Parcel No. 4</u> East half of Northeast quarter of Section Twenty-seven (27):

<u>Parcel No. 5</u> Lots numbered One (1) Two (2) and Three (3) of Section Twenty-seven (27):

<u>Excepting therefrom:</u>

1. A tract of One-fourth (¼) of an acre sold to George Murphy and bounded as follows: Beginning on Section line between Sections Twenty-six (26) and Twenty-seven (27) at north line of county road, running North on said line Two hundred (200) feet; thence West Fifty (50) feet; thence South Two Hundred (200) feet; thence East Fifty (50) feet to place of beginning.

2. Lots numbered Three (3) and Four (4) in Block Forty-six (46) of the proposed town of <u>Yahutes</u>, as originally plotted and recorded, said lots having been sold to O.V. Hurt.

<u>Parcel No. 6.</u> Northwest Quarter of Southwest Quarter of Section Twenty-Six (26):

<u>Excepting therefrom:</u>

1. A tract of One and One-half (1½) acres in Southwest corner of that part lying north of County Road and One-half (½) acre used as a school house site:

2. A tract of land described as follows: Commencing on the East and West subdivision line through the Southwest Quarter of Section Twenty-six (26) in Township Fourteen (14) South, Range Twelve (12) West, at a point fifty (50) feet East of the Southwest corner of the Northeast quarter of the Southwest quarter of said Section; thence running East on the subdivision line to a point at the intersection of said subdivision line and the North line of the County Road as now located; thence Southwesterly along the North line of said County Road to a point fifty (50) feet East from the North and South subdivision to said quarter section; thence North parallel with and fifty (50) feet from said North and South subdivision line to the place of beginning; being a triangular piece of land lying between the North line of the County Road and the South line of the Northeast quarter of the Southwest quarter of said Section Twenty-six (26) and containing about One (1) acre more or less.

Parcel No. 7. South half of South half of Section Twenty-six (26);

Parcel No. 8. Lot numbered Four (4) in Section Twenty-seven (27);

Parcel No. 9. Lots numbered One (1) and Two (2) in Section Thirty-four (34);

Parcel No. 10. Tract of about Three and Fifteen hundredths (3.15) acres from off the North side of Lot Three (3) in Section Thirty four (34); Beginning at Northwest corner of Northeast quarter of Southeast quarter of Section Thirty-four (34); thence running West along quarter line thirteen and Fourteen hundredths (13.14) chains to Pacific Ocean; thence South eighty (80) degrees, East Two and Ninety-nine hundredths (2.99) chains along the bank of said Ocean; thence South Eighty-five (85) degrees, Forty-five (45) minutes, East Twelve and Seventy-seven hundredths (12.77) chains to Eastern Boundary line of Lot numbered Three (3); thence North Two and Two hundredths (2.02) chains to place of beginning.

Excepting from the above described real property:

1. That certain tract of land laid out, platted and dedicated by Lumbermans Trust Company, an Oregon Corporation, as "Yachats", under date of July 31, 1923, which plat and dedication were recorded on August 2nd, 1923, in Book

6 at page 25 of the Plat Records of Lincoln County, State of Oregon.

2.. That certain tract of land laid out, platted and dedicated by Lumbermans Trust Company, an Oregon corporation, as "First Addition to Yachats", under date of July 10, 1926, which plat and dedication were recorded August 6th, 1926, in Book 7 at Page 14 of the Plat records of Lincoln County, State of Oregon.

2.. A strip of land Eighty (80) feet in width, being Forty (40) feet on either side of the center line of the Roosevelt Coast Highway, as now surveyed, said center line beginning at a point on the South line of Section Twenty-seven (27) in Township Fourteen (14) South, Range Twelve (12) West of Willamette Meridian, Two Hundred (200) feet West of the Southeast corner of said Section Twenty-seven (27), and being at Engineer's station 144 + 30 of said survey; thence running North 44° 35' East a distance of 750 feet more or less to station 151 + 50; thence in same direction a strip of land One Hundred (100) feet in width, being Fifty (50) feet on either side of said Center line of said survey a distance of 180 feet, more or less, to station 153 + 42.9; thence a like strip on a curve left with a radius of 458.4 feet a distance of 450 feet, more or less, to station 158 + 100; thence in a like curve left a strip of land Eighty (80) feet in width, being Forty (40) feet on either side of said center line of said survey a distance of 450 feet more or less to station 162 + 53.0; thence North 69° 11' West, a continuation of said Eighty (80) foot strip to the intersection of said center line with the South Line of First Street in the recorded plat of Yachats in said County of Lincoln, containing in all 4.17 acres, more or less.

All of said property being in Township Fourteen (14) South, of Ranger Twelve (12) West of the Willamette Meridian.

Parcel No. 11. Lots numbered Four (4) and Five (5) of Section Thirty-two (32) Township Eight (8) South, of Range Eleven (11 West of Willamette Meridian.

Excepting therefrom: a tract of land containing Five and Eighty-three hundredths (5.83) acres more or less, described in that certain deed from Lumbermans Trust Company, an Oregon Corporation, to the State of Oregon, to be held and maintained by it for public park purposes, dated January 19, 1926, and recorded March 5, 1926, in Book 49 at page 83 of the Deed Records of Lincoln County, State of Oregon.

And has also bargained and sold and by these presents does grant, bargain, sell and convey unto the said SIR ROBERT WILLIAM PERKS, the following described real property, situated in the County of Lincoln and State of Oregon, to-wit:

Lots Four (4) Eight (8), Nine (9) Ten (10) Thirteen (13) and Eighteen (18) and all of Lots Seven (7) and Fourteen (14) except a three-foot strip of land from off the West side of said Lots (7) and Fourteen (14), in <u>Block Two (2)</u>; Lots Two (2) Three (3) and Four (4) in <u>Block Three (3)</u>; Lot Four (4) in <u>Block Four (4)</u>; Lots One (1), Two (2), Three (3), Thirteen (13) and Fourteen (14) in <u>Block Seven (7)</u>; Lots One (1) and Fourteen (14) in <u>Block Eight (8)</u>, as shown in the official plat of Yachats, which plat is on file in the office of the County Recorder of Lincoln County, State of Oregon.

Lots One (1) to Twenty (20) both inclusive, and Lots Twenty-four (24) to Forty-two (42) both inclusive in Block One (1); Lots One(1) to Fourteen (14) both inclusive, and Lots Seventeen (17), Eighteen (18) Twenty-nine (29) Thirty (30), Thirty-one (31) Thirty-two (32), Thirty-three (33), Thirty-four (34), Tghirty-five (35), Thirty-six (36), Thirty-seven (37), Thirty-eight (38), Thirty-nine (39) and Forty (40) in <u>Block Two (2)</u>; Lots One (1) to Eighteen (18) both inclusive and Lots Twenty-nine (29), Thirty (30) and Thirty-one (31) in <u>Block Three (3)</u>; as shown in the official plat of First Addition to Yachats, which plat is on file in the office of the County Recorder of Lincoln County, State of Oregon.

Together with all and singular the tenements, hereditaments and appurtenances thereunto belonging or in anywise appertaining, and also all its estate, right, title, and interest in and to the same, including and together with all the Granter's right, title and interest in and to certain waters of Spruce Spring acquired, or to be acquired, through application No. 1043 and Permit No. 6989 issued by the State Engineer of the State of Oregon, to George Frost.

TO HAVE AND TO HOLD the above described and granter premises unto the said SIR ROBERT WILLIAM PERKS, his heirs and assigns forever.

IN WITNESS WHEREOF, LUMBERMANS TRUST COMPANY, the granter above named, has caused these presents to be executed by its proper officers thereunto duly authorized and its corporate seal to be hereto affixed, the 9th. Day of May, 1927.

Witnesses: LUMBERMANS TRUST COMPANY

John F. Sedgwick   By____C. Detering_____
                                       Vice President

Anne McNab   LUMBERMANS TRUST COMPANY

(CORPORATE SEAL) By____W. P. Briggs_____
                                       Secretary

STATE OF OREGON   )
) ss.
COUNTY OF MULTNOMAH)

    On this 9th. Day of May 1927, before me, a Notary Public, personally appeared C. DETERING and W. P. BRIGGS, both to me personally known, who being duly sworn did swear that he, the said C. DETERING is the Vice President, and he, the said W. P. BRIGGS is the Secretary, of LUMBERMANS TRUST COMPANY, the within named corporation, and that the seal affixed to said instrument is the corporate seal of said corporation, and that the said instrument was signed and sealed in behalf of said Corporation by authority of its Board of Directors, and said C. DETERING and W. P. BRIGGS acknowledged said instrument to be the free act and deed of said corporation.

    IN TESTIMONY WHEREOF, I have hereunto set my hand and affixed my official seal this, the day and year first in this, my certificate, written.

                                       Anne McNab

(NOTARIAL SEAL)   Notary Public for Oregon
                      My Commission Expires Feb. 25, 1929.

FILED AND RECORDED November 4th. 1927 at 2:34 o'clock P.M.

                              Carl Gildersleeve, County Clerk

By. Tilla Gildersleeve (signed) . . . . Deputy.

9 May 1927 - Sir Robert William Perks and Lady Edith Perks selling to the Equitable Trust Company (the renamed Lumbermans Trust).

A 12451

DEED

KNOW ALL MEN BY THESE PRESENTS, that SIR ROBERT WILLIAM PERKS and LADY EDITH PERKS, husband and wife, of London, England, in consideration of Ten Dollars ($ 10.00) and other valuable considerations to them paid by LUMBERMANS TRUST COMPANY, a corporation duly organizeds and existing under and by virtue of the laws of the State of Oregon, have bargained and sold, by these presents do grant, bargain, sell and convey unto said LUMBERMANS TRUST COMPANY, its successors and assigns, all the following bounded and described real property, situated in the County of Lincoln and State of Oregon, to-wit:

>   Parcel No: 1. Lot numbered Three (3) in section Twenty two (22);
>   Parcel No. 2 Southwest quarter of Southwest quarter (SW ¼ SW¼)of Section Three (23):
>   Parcel No. 3 West half of Northwest quarter (W½ NW¼) of Section Twenty-six (26):
>   Parcel No. 4 East half of Northeast quarter (E½ NE¼) of Section Twenty-seven (27):
>   Parcel No. 5 Lots numbered One (1) Two (2) and Three (3) of Section Twenty-seven (27):

Excepting therefrom:

    1. A tract of One-fourth (¼) of an acre sold to George Murphy and bounded as follows: Beginning on Section line between Sections Twenty-six (26) and Twenty-seven (27) at north line of county road, running North on said line Two hundred (200) feet; thence West Fifty (50) feet; thence South Two Hundred (200) feet; thence East Fifty (50) feet to place of beginning.

2. Lots numbered Three (3) and Four (4) in Block Forty-six (46) of the proposed town of <u>Yahutes</u>, as originally plotted and recorded, said lots having been sold to O.V. Hurt.

<u>Parcel No. 6.</u> Northwest Quarter of Southwest Quarter of Section Twenty-Six (26):

Excepting therefrom:

1. A tract of One and One-half (1½) acres in Southwest corner of that part lying north of County Road and One-half (½) acre used as a school house site:

2. A tract of land described as follows: Commencing on the East and West subdivision line through the Southwest Quarter of Section Twenty-six (26) in Township Fourteen (14) South, Range Twelve (12) West, at a point fifty (50) feet East of the Southwest corner of the Northeast quarter of the Southwest quarter of said Section; thence running East on the subdivision line to a point at the intersection of said subdivision line and the North line of the County Road as now located; thence Southwesterly along the North line of said County Road to a point fifty (50) feet East from the North and South subdivision to said quarter section; thence North parallel with and fifty (50) feet from said North and South subdivision line to the place of beginning; being a triangular piece of land lying between the North line of the County Road and the South line of the Northeast quarter of the Southwest quarter of said Section Twenty-six (26) and containing about One (1) acre more or less.

Parcel No. 7. South half of South half (S½ of S½)of Section Twenty-six (26);

Parcel No. 8. Lot numbered Four (4) in Section Twenty-seven (27);
Parcel No. 9. Lots numbered One (1) and Two (2) in Section Thirty-four (34);

Parcel No. 10. Tract of about Three and Fifteen hundredths (3.15) acres from off the North side of Lot Three (3) in Section Thirty four (34); Beginning at Northwest corner of Northeast quarter of Southeast quarter of Section Thirty-four (34); thence running West along quarter line thirteen and Fourteen hundredths (13.14) chains to Pacific Ocean; thence South eighty (80) degrees, East Two and Ninety-nine hundredths (2.99) chains along the bank of said Ocean; thence South Eighty-five (85) degrees, Forty-five (45) minutes, East Twelve and Seventy-seven hundredths (12.77) chains to Eastern Boundary line of Lot numbered Three (3); thence North Two and Two hundredths (2.02) chains to place of beginning.

Excepting from the above described real property:

1. That certain tract of land laid out, platted and dedicated by Lumbermans Trust Company, an Oregon Corporation, as "Yachats", under date of July 31,

1923, which plat and dedication were recorded on August 2nd, 1923, in Book 6 at page 25 of the Plat Records of Lincoln County, State of Oregon.

2.. That certain tract of land laid out, platted and dedicated by Lumbermans Trust Company, an Oregon corporation, as "First Addition to Yachats", under date of July 10, 1926, which plat and dedication were recorded August6th, 1926, in Book 7 at Page 14 of the Plat records of Lincoln County, State of Oregon.

2.. A strip of land Eighty (80) feet in width, being Forty (40) feet on either side of the center line of the Roosevelt Coast Highway, as now surveyed, said center line beginning at a point on the South line of Section Twenty-seven (27) in Township Fourteen (14) South, Range Twelve (12) West of Willamette Meridian, Two Hundred (200) feet West of the Southeast corner of said Section Twenty-seven (27), and being at Engineer's station 144 + 30 of said survey; thence running North 44° 35' East a distance of 750 feet more or less to station 151 + 50; thence in same direction a strip of land One Hundred (100) feet in width, being Fifty (50) feet on either side of said Center line of said survey a distance of 180 feet, more or less, to station 153 + 42.9; thence a like strip on a curve left with a radius of 458.4 feet a distance of 450 feet, more or less, to station 158 + 100; thence in a like curve left a strip of land Eighty (80) feet in width, being Forty (40) feet on either side of said center line of said survey a distance of 450 feet more or less to station 162 + 53.0; thence North 69° 11' West, a continuation of said Eighty (80) foot strip to the intersection of said center line with the South Line of First Street in the recorded plat of Yachats in said County of Lincoln, containing in all 4.17 acres, more or less.

All of said property being in Township Fourteen (14) South, of Ranger Twelve (12) West of the Willamette Meridian.

Parcel No. 11. Lots numbered Four (4) and Five (5) of Section Thirty-two (32) Township Eight (8) South, of Range Eleven (11 West of Willamette Meridian.

Excepting therefrom: a tract of land containing Five and Eighty-three hundredths (5.83) acres more or less, described in that certain deed from Lumbermans Trust Company, an Oregon Corporation, to the State of Oregon, to be held and maintained by it for public park purposes, dated January 19, 1926, and recorded March 5, 1926, in Book 49 at page 83 of the Deed Records of Lincoln County, State of Oregon.

And has also bargained and sold and by these presents does grant, bargain, sell and convey unto the said SIR ROBERT WILLIAM PERKS, the following described real property, situated in the County of Lincoln and State of Oregon, to-wit:

Lots Four (4) Eight (8), Nine (9) Ten (10) Thirteen (13) and Eighteen (18) and all of Lots Seven (7) and Fourteen (14) except a three-foot strip of land from off the West side of said Lots (7) and Fourteen (14), in <u>Block Two (2)</u>; Lots Two (2) Three (3) and Four (4) in <u>Block Three (3)</u>; Lot Four (4) in <u>Block Four (4)</u>; Lots One (1), Two (2), Three (3), Thirteen (13) and Fourteen (14) in <u>Block Seven (7)</u>; Lots One (1) and Fourteen (14) in <u>Block Eight (8)</u>, as shown in the official plat of Yachats, which plat is on file in the office of the County Recorder of Lincoln County, State of Oregon.

Lots One (1) to Twenty (20) both inclusive, and Lots Twenty-four (24) to Forty-two (42) both inclusive in Block One (1); Lots One(1) to Fourteen (14) both inclusive, and Lots Seventeen (17), Eighteen (18) Twenty-nine (29) Thirty (30), Thirty-one (31) Thirty-two (32), Thirty-three (33), Thirty-four (34), Tghirty-five (35), Thirty-six (36), Thirty-seven (37), Thirty-eight (38), Thirty-nine (39) and Forty (40) in <u>Block Two (2)</u>; Lots One (1) to Eighteen (18) both inclusive and Lots Twenty-nine (29), Thirty (30) and Thirty-one (31) in <u>Block Three (3)</u>; as shown in the official plat of First Addition to Yachats, which plat is on file in the office of the County Recorder of Lincoln County, State of Oregon.

Together with all and singular the tenements, hereditaments and appurtenances thereunto belonging or in anywise appertaining, and also all its estate, right, title, and interest in and to the same, including and together with all the Granter's right, title and interest in and to certain waters of Spruce Spring acquired, or to be acquired, through application No. 1043 and Permit No. 6989 issued by the State Engineer of the State of Oregon, to George Frost.

TO HAVE AND TO HOLD the above described and granted premises unto the said LUMBERMANS TRUST COMPANY, it successors and assigns forever. And the grantor SIR ROBERT WILLIAM PERKS does covenant to and with LUMBERMANS TRUST COMPANY, the above named grantee, its successors and assigns, that he is lawfully seized in fee simple of the above granted premises, that the above granted premises are free from all incumbrances and he will and his heirs, executors and administrators shall, warrant and forever defend the above granted premises, and every part and parcel thereof, against the lawful claims and demands of all persons whomsoever.

INWITNESS WHEREOF, the grantors above named have hereunto set their hands and seals this 9th. Day of May, 1927.

Witnesses: Robt. Wm. Perks (Wax seal)

R. N Perks   Edith Perks   (Wax seal)

Thos. C. Barrett

H.PV/N.P.
~~DOMINION OF~~ GREAT BRITIAN)
) SS
City & COUNTY OF London   )

On this 9th. Day of July 1927, before me, a Notary Public, personally appeared SIR ROBERT WILLIAM PERKS and LADY EDITH PERKS, husband and wife, both to me personally known to be the identified persons named in and who executed the within instrument and acknowledged to me that they executed the ~~within instrument, and acknowledged to me that they executed the~~ same freely and voluntarily.

IN TESTIMONY WHEREOF, I have hereunto set my hand and affixed my Notarial seal the day and year first in this, my certificate, written.

                                H. Peter Venn

(NOTARIAL SEAL)   Not. Pub.
                              Notary Public in and for
                              London, England.
(Revenue Stamp cancelled)   (My Commission expires with life)
    One Shilling

FILED AND RECORDED November 4th. 1927 at 2:36 O'clock P. M.
                                      Carl Gildersleeve, County Clerk.

By Tilla Gildersleeve (sign). . . . Deputy

10 Sept 1929 - The Equitable Trust selling to the Oregon Conference Evangelical Church of Oregon.

A 16763

KNOW ALL MEN BY THESE PRESENTS, That Equitable Trust Company, a corporation duly organized and existing under and by virtue of the laws of the State of Oregon (whose corporate name was formerly Lumbermans Trust Company, but was changed to Equitable Trust Company, by supplementary articles of incorporation, duly filed and approved by the Superintendent of Banks of the State of Oregon, in consideration of Ten ($10.00) Dollars and no/100 Dollars, to it in hand paid by Board of Trustees, Oregon Conference Evangelical Church of Oregon, State of Oregon, has bargained and sold and by these presents does bargain and sell, grant and convey unto the said Board of Trustees, Oregon Conference Evangelical Church of Oregon, its successors and assigns, all the following bounded and described real property, situated in the County of Lincoln and State of Oregon, to-wit:

> All of Lot Twelve (12) in Block One (1), First Addition to Yachats, according to the duly recorded plat thereof on file in the office of the County Clerk in Lincoln County, State of Oregon.

Together with all and singular the tenements, hereditments and appurtenances thereto belonging or in anywise appertaining, and also all its right, title, estate and interest in and to the same.

TO HAVE AND TO HOLD the above described and granted premises unto the said Board of Trustees, Oregon Conference Evangelical Church of Oregon, its successors and assigns forever.

This conveyance is nevertheless upon the express conditions following:

FIRST. That the said property shall be used and maintained for religious purposes only.

SECOND. That a properly constructed septic tank shall be used and maintained in connection with all toilets and water closets now, on or which may hereafter be placed upon said premises, until such time as a proper sewage system shall be maintained in connection therewith.

THIRD. That no barns, stables, or pig pens shall be constructed, used, or maintained upon said premises.

In case of violation of the foregoing conditions to any of them, this conveyance shall thereupon become void and the title to said premises and the whole thereof shall revert to and revest in the grantor herein or its successors and assigns as of its first and former estate, and the grantor herein or its successors and assigns may re-enter and re-possess themselves of said premises as of its former estate as fully and completely as tough this conveyance had not been executed.

And the grantor above named does covenant to and with the above named grantee, its successors and assigns, that it will and its successors shall, warrant and forever defend the above granted premised and every part and parcel thereof, against the lawful demands of all persons whomsoever claiming through or under said grantor.

IN WITNESS WHEREOF, said grantor, by authority of its Board of Directors, has caused these present to be subscribed by its Vice President and Secretary and its corporate name and seal to be hereunto affixed this 10th day of September, 1929.

Signed, sealed and delivered
in the presence of: Equitable Trust Company

E. F. Paulsen   By Earl C. Bronaugh, President

R. E. Woodworth   (CORPORATE SEAL)   By W. P. Briggs, Secretary

STATE OF OREGON   )
) SS
COUNTY OF MULTNOMAH)

BE IT REMEMBERED, That on this 10th day of September, 1929, before me, the undersigned, a Notary Public in and for said County and State, personally appeared Earl C. Bronaugh and W. P. Briggs, both to me personally known and who, being first duly sworn, did say that he, the said Earl C. Bronaugh is the President, and he, the said W. F. Briggs, is the Secretary of Equitable Trust Company, and that the seal affixed to said instrument is the corporate seal of said corporation and that the instrument was signed and sealed in behalf of said corporation by authority of its Board of Directors, and they acknowledged said instrument to be the free act and deed of said corporation.

IN WITNESS WHEREOF, I have hereunto set my hand and affixed

my notarial seal the day and year first in this, my certificate, written.

        E. F. Paulsen
        Notary Public for Oregon
        My commission expires: Dec. 4,
(NOTARIAL SEAL)   1929.

FILED AND RECORDED September 18th, 1929 At 1:18 O'clock P.M.
        Carl Gildersleeve, County Clerk.

By Tilla Gildersleeve (sign) . . . Deputy

8 Aug 1952 - The Oregon Conference of Evangelical Church of Oregon selling to Willamette Presbytery Church.

Book 154 Page 89

WARRANTY DEED.

THIS INDENTURE WITNESSESTH: that OREGON-WASHINGTON CONFERENCE OF THE EVANGELICAL UNITED BRETHREN CHURCH, a corporation, successor to Board of Trustees, Oregon Conference Evangelical Church of Oregon, for the consideration of the sum of Ten and NO-DOLLARS, to it paid, had bargained and sold, and by these presents does grant, bargain, sell and convey unto Willamette Presbytery of the Presbyterian Church, U.S.A., its successors and assigns, the following described lands and premises, situated in the County of Lincoln and State of Oregon, to-wit:

> All of Lot Twelve (12) in Block One (1), First Addition to Yachats, according to the duly recorded plat thereof on file in the office of the County Clerk in Lincoln County, State of Oregon.

> SUBJECT to restrictions contained in deed from Equitable Trust Company, a corporation, to Board of Trustees, Oregon Confe3rence Evangelical Church of Oregon, recorded September 18, 1929, in the Deed Records of Lincoln County, Oregon.

TO HAVE AND TO HOLD the said premises, with their appurtenances, unto the said Willamette Presbytery of the Presbyterian Church, U..A., its successors and assigns forever.

And said Oregon-Washington Conference of the Evangelical United Brethren Church, a corporation, does hereby covenant to and with the said grantee, its successors and assigns, that it is the owner in fee simple of said premises: that they are free from all encumbrances and that it will warrant and defend the same from all lawful claims whatsoever, except as hereinabove provided.

IN TESTIMONY WHEREOF, Oregon-Washington Conference of the Evangelical United Brethren Church, a corporation, has caused its corporate seal to be affixed and these presents to be subscribed by the President and Secretary of its Board of Trustees, the 8th day of August, 1952..

(CORPORATE SEAL) OREGON-WASHINGTON CONFERENCE OF THE EVANGELICAL UNITED BRETHREN CHURCH, a Corporation,

By _____(Signed)_____ President
By _____(Signed)_____ Secretary
    Of Board of Trustees.

About the Author

George R. Mead began to study anthropology in 1962 after being discharged (honorably) from the U. S. Army, Combat Engineers. He eventually received his degrees, a B.A., a M. A., and a Ph. D. in his chosen field. And many years later an M. S. W. in Clinical Social Work. He has worked in aerospace, taught at the college and university levels, worked in a community action agency, ran a restaurant, been unemployed, and worked for the U. S. Forest Service. He is now retired from the work-a-day world but does a certain amount of consulting, writing, and research. He lives seven miles outside of the small town of La Grande, Oregon, with his wife, two cats, and one dog. Rez joined the house as an eight-week old puppy found by Katy, a German Shepard (now deceased) under some brush in the middle of the American Southwest desert. Rez is now weighs 92 pounds (some puppy).

www.ingramcontent.com/pod-product-compliance
Lightning Source LLC
Chambersburg PA
CBHW071409040426
42444CB00009B/2172